The Guide to Remy's World

Disney · PIXAR
RATATOUILLE
(rat·a·too·ee)

The Guide to Remy's World

Written by Glenn Dakin

Contents

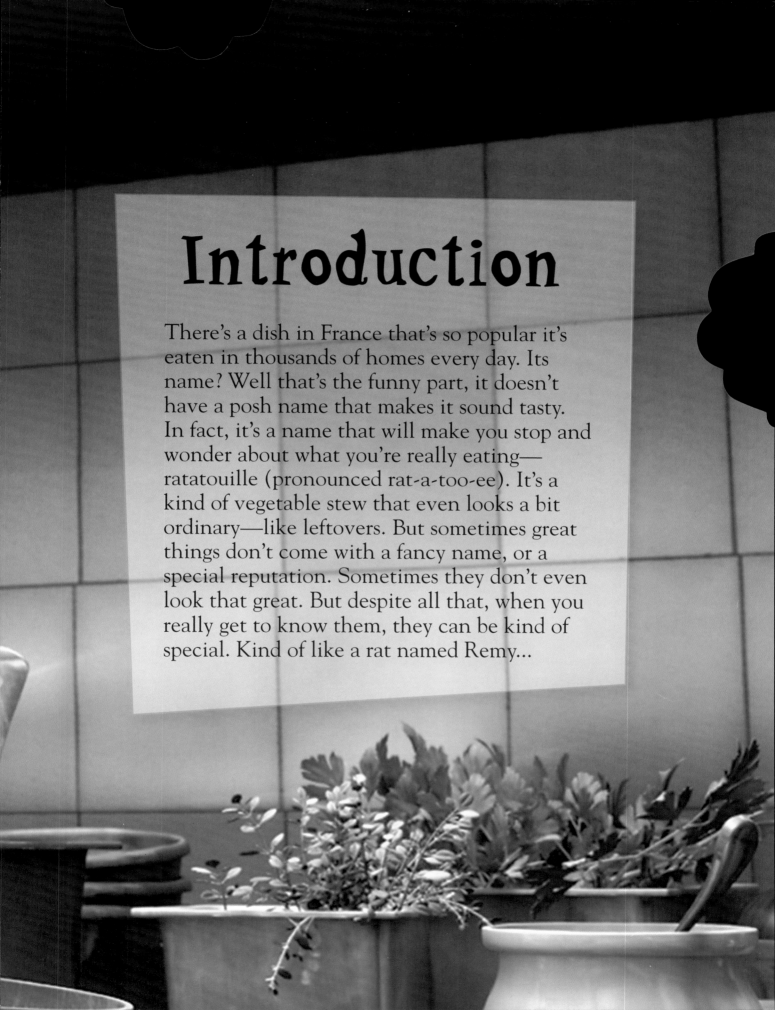

Introduction

There's a dish in France that's so popular it's eaten in thousands of homes every day. Its name? Well that's the funny part, it doesn't have a posh name that makes it sound tasty. In fact, it's a name that will make you stop and wonder about what you're really eating— ratatouille (pronounced rat-a-too-ee). It's a kind of vegetable stew that even looks a bit ordinary—like leftovers. But sometimes great things don't come with a fancy name, or a special reputation. Sometimes they don't even look that great. But despite all that, when you really get to know them, they can be kind of special. Kind of like a rat named Remy...

Remy

Ears are alert for sounds of approaching humans.

Super-sensitive nose is Remy's most valuable asset.

Remy is a culinary genius. He should have a bright future ahead as a chef, but there's just one problem—he's a rat. However, this small rodent has some big ideas and there's no way Remy is going to spend his life eating garbage like the rest of his family. He is determined to become a proper chef.

Remy is a natural when it comes to seeking out the finest of ingredients. Like his hero, Gusteau, his favorite spice is saffron.

Standing on his hind legs keeps his front paws clean.

Radical Idea

Unlike other rats, Remy thinks he could learn a lot from humans. Humans don't just survive, they discover and create—especially in the kitchen! Remy is already in touch with his human side, he walks upright to keep his paws clean enough to cook.

It's not easy being a chef when most of the ingredients are bigger than you are! At least they provide a good hiding place...

The Smell of Success

With his highly developed sense of taste and smell, Remy is a master of combining flavors. Although this puts him head and shoulders above most human chefs, in rat society his gift is only useful for one thing—sniffing out rat poison.

Remy's the crème de la crème of rats!

crème liquide

"Everyone likes my cooking!"

Master Chef

Remy's idol is the great French chef, Auguste Gusteau. Gusteau's famous cookbook *Anyone Can Cook!* is Remy's prized possession. Remy dreams of becoming a famous chef, just like Gusteau.

Remy Facts

J'adore
- Studying Gusteau's cookbook
- Convincing my brother Emile that food is tastier than garbage
- Getting creative in the kitchen

Je déteste
- Being a poison checker
- Eating unidentifiable garbage
- Having dirty paws— it's so unhygienic!

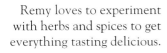

Like all rats, Remy loves cheese. However, he prefers to eat fine cheeses such as Brie, Roquefort, Camembert, and Emmenthal.

Remy loves to experiment with herbs and spices to get everything tasting delicious.

Emile always has a cheerful smile.

Emile

Remy's younger brother, Emile, is a friendly fur ball. According to Remy, Emile's best quality is that he is easily impressed. Although Emile can't understand why his brother walks on two legs and washes his paws before eating, he still believes that Remy has a unique talent.

Garbage Gourmet

Like Remy, Emile loves his food, but unlike his brother he will eat anything. Literally. Remy tries to teach Emile how to appreciate fine flavors, but Emile is just as happy munching on unidentified garbage.

Emile is always happiest when his belly is full.

This might look like an ordinary garbage can, but to Emile it's an all-night diner—full of tasty treats and decomposing delicacies.

Emile Facts

J'adore
- Hanging out with my little brother (and I mean size, not years)
- Eating. Anything
- No really...anything

Je déteste
- Making Dad mad
- Losing Remy
- Being hungry
- Lightning!

Brotherly Love
Remy needs a pal to share his secrets with. Only Emile knows that Remy is obsessed with the world of humans and dreams of being a chef.

Thick and Thin
Emile is always telling Remy that they shouldn't be sneaking into Mabel's kitchen. However, he is always ready to support Remy—even if his brother tries to involve him in "criminal" activities such as reading books and watching TV.

"This is not good!"

Here Comes Trouble
For Emile, following his older brother anywhere has its downsides. Like being caught stealing in the kitchen of an elderly woman with a shotgun...

Django

Remy and Emile's father, Django, is the leader of the rat colony. Django's only goal in life is to protect his rats, especially his beloved sons. He believes that humans are dangerous and that rats should stay away from them.

Bushy eyebrows make Django look like he means business!

Extra-long nose makes Django stand out from the rest of the rat colony

Big Daddy

This streetwise survivor insists that rats aren't thieves because they only take stuff that no-one wants. Django has trained his rat pack to be a sophisticated garbage collection service.

Rat Pack

Django is the guy in charge when it comes to his extended rat family. He will do anything in his power to make sure no rat comes in contact with a human.

Emile is Django's low-maintenance son. Unlike Remy, he never questions Django, and won't bring shame on his father by trying to be human-like.

Fatherly Advice

Remy's father believes that being picky about food is a recipe for disaster. According to Django, food is just fuel, and if you're too fussy you won't last long in the real world.

"Shut up and eat your garbage!"

Django Facts

J'adore

- Living life the traditional rat way
- Gypsy music
- Securing a safe haven for the rat clan

Je déteste

- Humans—they are bad news for rats
- Being called a thief
- Losing a son

Despite their differences, deep down Django knows that Remy is a very talented rat.

The Cottage

Remy's home is a charming cottage situated in the countryside, just on the outskirts of Paris, France. It belongs to a short-sighted old lady named Mabel who has no idea that she has a whole colony of rats living in her attic.

The rats live happily in the attic amongst Mabel's old junk.

Tough Lady
She may look like a frail old lady, but Mabel has history. She fought for the French resistance in World War 2 and knows how to protect herself— even against rats!

The Kitchen

Mabel's antique kitchen is a treasure trove for rats. Remy enjoys sniffing out the herbs and spices in her cupboards, while Emile just likes finding scraps of moldy food.

The cottage has traditional French shuttered windows.

Poison Checker

While Mabel sleeps inside the cottage, Remy is busy outside being a poison checker. His job is to make sure the food scraps are safe enough for the rats to eat!

15

Evacuate!

Remy's dangerous habit of rummaging for spices in the kitchen while Mabel snores watching TV, eventually leads to disaster for the rats. Happening to glance at the TV, Remy is shocked to learn that his hero Gusteau is dead. When Mabel wakes and catches sight of a rat, it's time for Remy to make a quick exit!

Remy ignores Django and Emile's advice and follows his nose instead. His quest for some saffron for his latest culinary concoction is one daring step too far.

Recipe for Disaster
Mabel's reaction to her unwelcome guests is to blast them with a shotgun, which reveals their attic hiding place. The rats soon realize they are no longer safe in their cozy cottage.

Sewer Scramble
Led by Django, the rats evacuate to the sewer to regroup and look for a new home. Luckily, making a fast exit is what rats do best. Building boats out of whatever they can find, they hit the river and the safety of a storm drain.

Quick Getaway

Only one of the rats gets lost in the panic. Remy couldn't bear to leave Gusteau's cookbook behind at the cottage, but when he goes back to get it, he becomes separated from the rest of the pack.

All Alone

Remy is left floating down the sewer on his prized possession. Although the book probably saves his life, he may never see Emile or Django again.

Gourmet City

Paris, France's glamorous capital city welcomes all lovers of good food— apart from rats of course. To Remy, every glowing light represents a warm café or cozy kitchen where he isn't wanted. But this city has a history of daring to accept new fashions and new ideas. Perhaps for a unique talent like Remy, anything is possible...

Could Paris be the city of opportunity for a rat like Remy?

Alone in Paris

Gusteau's hat is on display at his famous Paris restaurant.

There are many ways to discover the wonderful city of Paris, but emerging from a damp sewer, having just lost your family and friends isn't top of the list! Remy now has to tackle life's problems alone… or does he? Is it just his crazy imagination, or is there a friendly spirit to guide him?

Guiding Light

An imaginary friend is better than no friend at all, especially when you're in trouble. Gusteau assures a starving Remy that "food will always come to those who love to cook."

Remy sees Paris like no tourist can, traveling inside walls, through ceilings, and across floors. Along the way he catches glimpses of how Parisians live. For Remy it is a true behind-the-scenes journey.

Remy is thrilled when Gusteau's advice leads him to a place he has always dreamed of. Surely, it must be destiny that has brought Remy to the front of his hero's world-famous restaurant.

The Promised Land
Wide-eyed and quivery-whiskered, Remy thrills to the sights, sounds, and smells of *Gusteau's* famous, bustling kitchen. It would be a dream come true to cook alongside such world-class chefs!

Like many top chefs, Gusteau enjoyed eating almost as much as cooking!

Remy should be more careful about walking on rooftops. He loses his balance and takes a plunge into the kitchen below. It's one massive leap for ratkind—straight into human territory!

Paws spread in standard rat panic position

Chopping board—a nasty landing place

Danger Zone
A kitchen is a cozy place for humans, but it's a deadly assault course for a rat. Remy must dodge hot pots, sharp knives, and flaming stove tops. His biggest obstacles are the thundering feet of towering chefs!

Sponge=a soft landing!

No Place For a Rat

Remy is overjoyed when he finds himself poised above *Gusteau's* famous kitchen with a perfect view of all its delights. But the dream turns into a nightmare when the skylight he's looking through suddenly gives way and sends him plunging into danger. Up above, he was an appreciative observer, but down below he's a kitchen's worst enemy—a RAT.

Remy begins his terrifying trip with a plunge into greasy dishwater. Luckily he paddles to the surface, and hopes to make a clean getaway.

Metal surface, ouch!

Splash down in the sink—don't worry, rats are excellent swimmers.

Gusteau's comes close to getting a new dish on the menu—flambéed rat. When Remy tries to scurry across a kitchen floor to safety, a busy chef unknowingly makes things hot for him.

When Remy plans to escape from the kitchen, he gets distracted and starts imagining various ways he could fix a disastrous soup.

Pots, pans, and colanders make handy traps for a rodent on-the-run. When kitchen boy, Linguini, traps Remy under a colander, it is the start of a cooking adventure for both of them.

In a Jam

It's nearly the end of the line when Remy's trapped in a jar. Head Chef Skinner wants to dispose of the unwelcome guest. Luckily, kitchen boy Linguini has other ideas...

Bonjour!

Designing a restaurant is an art. Lights must be charmingly low, but not dark and gloomy, while the kitchen must be simple, efficient, and hygienic. *Gusteau's*, of course, combines all of these qualities, and the food is beyond compare.

Every table is laid with a spotless white tablecloth, a bouquet of fresh flowers, and fine silver cutlery.

Foyer

Dining Room

Head Chef, Skinner, has kept Gusteau's old office as he left it, except for some large cardboard cutouts of his gourmet microwaveable munchies.

The food safe could be a very tempting place for a hungry rat!

Gusteau's prides itself on not just making food, but making food with flair!

Kitchen

Courtyard

The pass is the staging point for all dinner orders and finished dishes, so waiters can satisfy their hungry customers.

Gusteau's

Bienvenue! *Gusteau's* is one of Paris's oldest and most famous restaurants. With its sophisticated décor and soft lighting, it's no surprise this eatery features the best chefs in town. Even the waiters are professionals, making sure every fork is in line and every napkin is folded to perfection. Bon appétit!

Bouquet of fresh flowers

Plush velvet chairs

Ready to Serve
Head Waiter, Mustafa, makes sure that the customers are satisfied at all times. He is a vital link between the dining room and the kitchen—taking compliments to the chef and delivering the news that the customers are demanding new creations...

Elegant crystal chandeliers

Crisp, white tablecloths

When Mustafa grabs for a dish off a passing trolley, he ends up with a handful of rat instead. Luckily Remy escapes before Mustafa ____ the full furry facts!

The new garbage boy is about to make a surprising mark on *Gusteau's*. Perhaps he will bring back a five-star rating to the restaurant with his innovative ideas...

The Kitchen

To the customers, a restaurant kitchen is a place of magic and mystery, where delicious dreams are brought to life, but to the busy chefs it is a steaming battle-zone, where one slip-up can spell disaster. A kitchen is a miniature empire, where hapless chefs are bossed about by a screaming tyrant whose every word is law. Well, at least one works that way...

Team Work

There's no time for slacking in this kitchen. The chefs work morning to night peeling, chopping, slicing, dicing, roasting, and toasting—sticking faithfully to the recipes in Gusteau's *Anyone Can Cook!*

The Food Chain

The key to running a successful restaurant is organization. In *Gusteau's* kitchen everyone knows exactly what he or she is supposed to be doing.

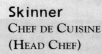

Skinner
CHEF DE CUISINE (HEAD CHEF)

As the boss, Skinner's job is to tell everyone what to do. He loves feeling superior—well it's nice for the pint-sized chef to have people looking up to him for a change!

Horst
SOUS CHEF (ASSISTANT TO HEAD CHEF)

Being Skinner's deputy is a tough job, but Horst can handle it. Everyone knows he's been in prison—for fraud, or bank robbery or making a hole in the ozone layer over Avignon. (He changes the story every time he tells it!)

Colette
CHEF DE PARTIE (MEAT AND POULTRY CHEF)

The toughest cook in the kitchen. No man would dare to get in her way!

Pompidou
PATISSIER (PASTRY CHEF)

An independent worker who likes to gamble, but he would never take a chance with *Gusteau's* reputation.

Lalo
POISSONIER (FISH CHEF)

This hot-shot knows how to sauté, although he actually ran away from home to be an acrobat.

Larousse
GARDE MANGER (SALAD AND APPETIZER CHEF)

This quiet chef knows how to prepare a winning salad.

Linguini
PLONGEUR/COMMIS (GARBAGE BOY/PREP COOK)

This bottom-of-the-food-chain garbage boy goes from sweeping floors to chopping vegetables. It would be a miracle for a guy like him to become a top chef in this cutthroat kitchen.

Linguini

Linguini is Gusteau's son and the true heir to his restaurant, but his mother, Renata, never told him. Linguini gives Skinner a letter containing Renata's dying request—that he be given a job at *Gusteau's*. Although he is given the worst job in the whole place, Linguini's luck could be about to change...

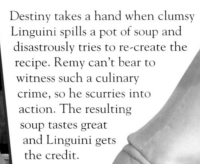

Destiny takes a hand when clumsy Linguini spills a pot of soup and disastrously tries to re-create the recipe. Remy can't bear to witness such a culinary crime, so he scurries into action. The resulting soup tastes great and Linguini gets the credit.

Garbage Boy

Linguini means well but somehow he never keeps a job for very long. This time he is determined to keep his job at *Gusteau's*. He has no idea who he reall is, and he never will if Skinner has anything to do with it.

Pride and Joy

Linguini's trusty bike might lack style and it barely fits into his tiny apartment, but it is perfect for zipping around the streets of Paris.

The paintwork is chipped and flaking.

Well-used traditional yarn-head mop

Turned-in feet prevent slipping on mopped floor

These old tires have seen better days.

Le Morning After
After an evening of fine wines and a cozy chat with Skinner, Linguini falls asleep on the job. The sneaky boss wanted to get Linguini drunk in order to find out about the rat he's been seeing. But Linguini isn't about to rat on his rodent partner.

Meeting Remy offers Linguini the chance to move up in the world. Instead of getting rid of him, Linguini forms a unique team with the clever rat. After all, two heads are better than one—especially when it comes to cooking.

" Let's do this thing! "

New Chef
Linguini goes from maestro of the mop to a culinary success, thanks to Remy. But how can this unusual pair ever hope to fool Skinner?

Remy has to teach Linguini how to chop vegetables.

Linguini Facts

J'adore
- Cooking, with Remy's help
- Admiring Colette's cute scowl
- Inheriting a fortune and a top restaurant

Je déteste
- Being fired from a job
- Little rat feet running up and down my back
- Having my love life managed by a rat

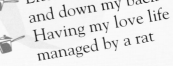

Skinner

After years of working for Gusteau, Skinner's own recipe for success is to let the restaurant run itself, while he cooks up get-rich-quick schemes. He's turned the restaurant, once a center of culinary art, into a profitable but soulless luxury meal machine. His long-term plan is to inherit the restaurant, as long as no heir turns up to claim it…

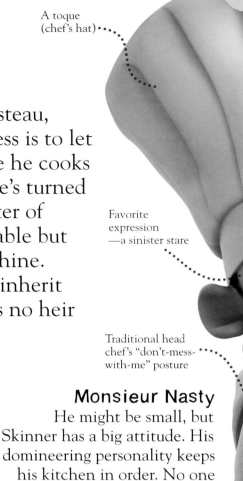

A toque (chef's hat)

Favorite expression —a sinister stare

Traditional head chef's "don't-mess-with-me" posture

Monsieur Nasty

He might be small, but Skinner has a big attitude. His domineering personality keeps his kitchen in order. No one dares to criticize him or his tasteless business ideas.

Skinner is furious when Linguini's soup is a hit, but he tries not to show it. If Linguini wants to try his luck at the fine art of cooking, then who is Skinner to stand in his way? After all, he'll enjoy watching Linguini fail.

When Linguini continues to be a hit in the kitchen, Skinner is outraged. He is worried that a cool new chef will ruin his plans to use Gusteau's face on all his cheap and tacky snack products.

Skinner Facts

J'adore

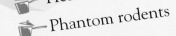
- Being the boss
- Inventing bite-sized and batter-dipped frozen foods
- Setting rat-traps

Je déteste
- Ambitious plongeurs
- Heir-raising letters
- Phantom rodents

A step ladder is a vital aid for a vertically-challenged snooper. The sneaky chef anxiously awaits a customer's reaction to Linguini's soup creation.

Don't Look Now...

Skinner keeps on catching glimpses of the elusive Remy, but he can't quite believe his eyes! His trademark stare is becoming increasingly wild—is he losing his mind?

" You're fired! "

Skinner is sure that he can hear strange noises...

Hat Trick

Head chef Skinner's toque appears extra-tall, due to his short stature. Sadly, its impressive height doesn't make up for his low-down attitude.

Heavily starched to stand as tall as possible

The Rodent Conspiracy Theory works like this—on Linguini's first day Skinner ordered him to kill a rat. Since then, Skinner keeps seeing Linguini with a rat, but he can never quite catch them. Skinner believes that Linguini must be taunting him, by making him think that the rat is important in some way.

The food safe is the last place any chef would expect to find a rat. So, naturally, that's where Skinner tries to catch Linguini talking to his rat friend.

Colette

Only one woman works at *Gusteau's*. In order to make it in a macho world, Colette has to be the toughest chef in the kitchen. She is clever, focused, and determined to succeed in the male-dominated world of gourmet cuisine.

Master Plan

The secret of Colette's survival at one of Paris's top restaurants is always following the recipe. She never deviates from Gusteau's recipes, not even by a single cuttlefish tentacle.

Short, chic bob

Cooking utensils should always be clean.

Colette is so dedicated that she is often the first person to arrive in the morning and the last one to leave at night. All she has ever wanted to be is a good chef.

A mark of a true chef is to always have clean sleeves.

Colette Facts

J'adore
- Riding a motorcycle
- Always following the recipe
- People who listen
- Cute garbage boys

Je déteste
- Gusteau's veal stomach special
- Guys who keep secrets
- Stale bread

Girl's Best Friend

Colette's wheels are very different from Linguini's! She loves her sleek, powerful motorcycle and it's great if she needs to make a fast exit. There's also plenty of room on the back to take her *cheri* (and his rat pal) for a spin around Paris.

Side mirrors are ideal for checking out fellow passengers.

Every Parisian girl learns how to strike a cool pose.

Colette saves Linguini's job when Skinner wants to fire him for adding his own je-ne-sais-quoi to the soup. He may be a pan-scrubber but she reminds everyone that Gusteau's most cherished belief was that "anyone can cook".

Skinner insists that Colette take a personal interest in Linguini's career after she stands up for him. He gives her the job of teaching Linguini how to cook, with some surprising results.

"Follow the recipe!"

Sweet Music

Colette can tell how fresh bread is just by the sound of the crust. To her trained ear, a good loaf will produce a symphony of crackles.

The Little Chef

Every famous chef has his or her inspiration—maybe a famous mentor or a signature style—but Linguini is different. To the outside world he's a young culinary genius, but sitting snugly (and invisibly) under his hat is a tiny secret—a talented rodent who guides every move Linguini makes in the kitchen.

Remy and Linguini are happy to be a team.

By the banks of the River Seine, Remy and Linguini form a partnership. Linguini needs help to keep his job in *Gusteau's* kitchen, and Remy wants the chance to follow his dreams and become a real chef.

Remy rarely gets the chance to be a paws-on chef. However, at home in Linguini's apartment he's free to rustle up a tasty omelette because no one is around to stare.

Double Act

Like steak and frites, these two are the perfect combination. Remy has a talent for cooking but the wrong look for the kitchen, while Linguini looks the part (well, he's human!) but he is a hopeless chef.

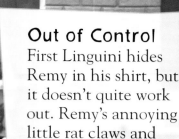

Out of Control

First Linguini hides Remy in his shirt, but it doesn't quite work out. Remy's annoying little rat claws and painful bites convince Linguini that the team needs a new plan.

"Neither of us can do this alone!"

Right hair pull controls right arm. Check!

Remy, hiding under Linguini's toque, stumbles onto something. Pulling Linguini's hair saves them from a collision with Mustafa and a pile of dirty dishes. This involuntary control system could be the perfect solution!

Hours of cooking practice turn the daring duo into a lean, mean, haute-cuisine machine! Okay, so one time, Linguini did accidentally hurl a pan out of his apartment window...

Linguini anxiously awaits the verdict.

It's a tense moment when Skinner tests Remy's soup. The boss pulls a disgusted face but the truth is, it's delicious. But how long will it be before Linguini's little secret is discovered?

What's Cooking?

They say that Paris is the most romantic city in the world, and they also say that the way to someone's heart is through their stomach. Working side by side, day after day, in the passionate, hectic atmosphere of *Gusteau's* kitchen, perhaps Linguini and Colette were bound to discover the perfect recipe for love.

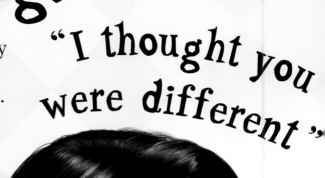

"I thought you were different"

Chopping vegetables together may not be a typical first date but this cordon bleu couple isn't complaining. Colette is convinced that Linguini is different from other men—for one thing, when you give him advice he actually takes it!

Colette

Proving she's tough enough to make it in a man's world leaves Colette little time for romance. That's until a clumsy-but-sweet young chef spices up her life…

A passionate French heart lurks beneath the chef's uniform.

Typically tough posture, but Colette has a secret soft side.

It sure hurts if the guy you love snores in your face when you're pouring your heart out to him. Colette just wants to smack some sense into that superstar-in-shades act. After all, she taught the boy everything he knows.

Rodent romantic
advisor (concealed) ·········

Sometimes one tiny secret can ruin a budding
relationship—in this case the tiny secret just
happens to have whiskers and a tail! When
Colette threatens to ride away, Linguini
realizes it's time to tell her the truth...

Cutely confused
···· look—can melt
hearts

"I love you...rrr...advice"

Linguini
Linguini knows as much about love
as he does about soup. Luckily, his
secret deal with Remy makes him
appear more talented and
mysterious than he really is!

Linguini isn't very good with words. He isn't very
good at cooking either. Come to think of it, his
mopping wasn't great. In the end, Remy helps
Linguini get his feelings across to Colette—with
a kiss that surprises them both!

Skinner's Plans

A man like Skinner didn't get where he is today without a cunning scheme or two. He'd think up anything to get his two greatest loves—money and power—and anyone who gets in his way should watch out! In fact, Skinner is ready to serve up a whole bunch of trouble for poor Linguini.

Cashing In

Skinner plans to exploit Chef Gusteau's famous face by launching a range of snack products. Microwave burritos and pizza top his list of must-have munchies. Gusteau would not have been impressed!

Marketing Madness

Advertising guru Francois Dupuis loves thinking up cheesy slogans as much as Skinner loves inventing cheap snacks. One of his classics is "Gusteau makes Chinese food Chine-easy".

Every new snack range comes with a corny makeover for poor Gusteau.

Dupuis' tacky ideas make him the perfect businessman for Skinner.

For a new "corn puppies" campaign Dupuis and Skinner have sunk to an all-time low—Gusteau will be portrayed as a big ear of corn in doggie make-up!

Skinner hopes to find out the secret of Linguini's success and ruin the budding chef's reputation. There must be more to this garbage boy than meets the eye! Spying and creeping about come naturally to the horrific head chef.

Gusteau's will states that if an heir doesn't turn up within 2 years, Skinner will inherit the restaurant. When Skinner reads Renata's letter claiming that Linguini is Gusteau's son, it is only a month until the deadline so Skinner tries to hide the truth until it's too late.

Skinner refuses to let a garbage boy ruin his carefully-laid plans!

Dirty Trick
When he discovers Linguini's secret, Skinner dishes up his meanest plan of all—calling in the dreaded Health Inspector to check *Gusteau's* for a rat infestation.

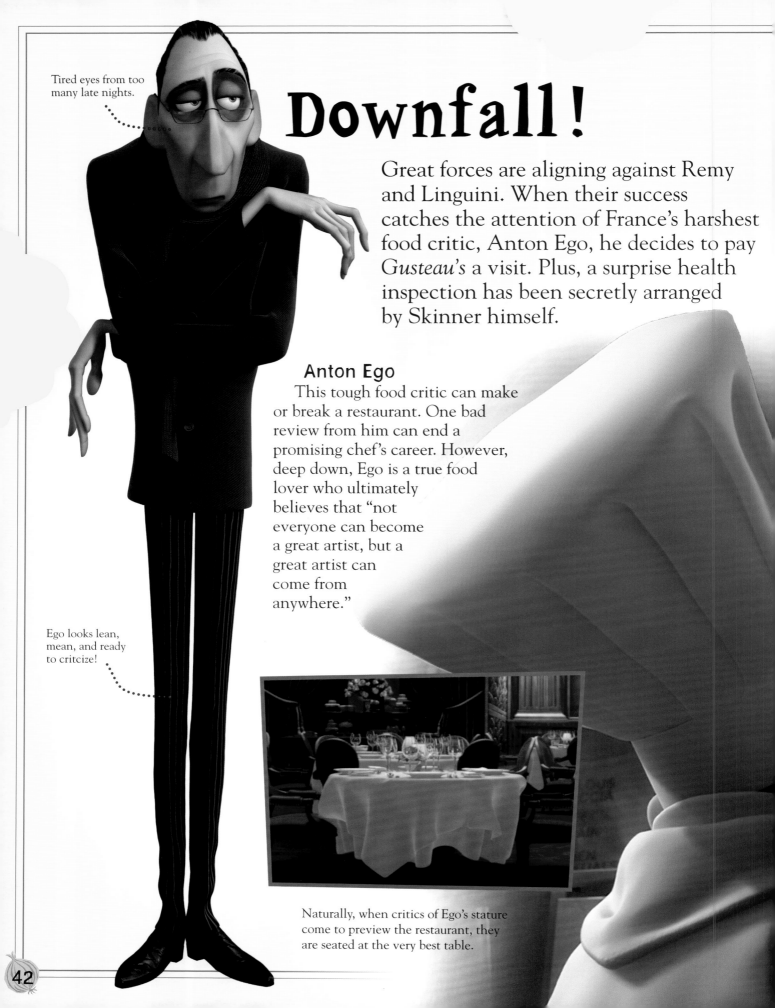

Tired eyes from too
many late nights.

Downfall!

Great forces are aligning against Remy
and Linguini. When their success
catches the attention of France's harshest
food critic, Anton Ego, he decides to pay
Gusteau's a visit. Plus, a surprise health
inspection has been secretly arranged
by Skinner himself.

Anton Ego

This tough food critic can make
or break a restaurant. One bad
review from him can end a
promising chef's career. However,
deep down, Ego is a true food
lover who ultimately
believes that "not
everyone can become
a great artist, but a
great artist can
come from
anywhere."

Ego looks lean,
mean, and ready
to critcize!

Naturally, when critics of Ego's stature
come to preview the restaurant, they
are seated at the very best table.

When Ego orders the house speciality, he has no idea what culinary delights Remy and Linguini have in store for him. What will the clever critic have to say?

Skinner also hopes his cunning lawyer, Talon Labarthe, might have good news, but a DNA test on a strand of Linguini's hair proves that he really is Gusteau's son.

Hairy Problem

There is one mystery that Labarthe cannot explain— the first results of the DNA analysis found that the hair plucked from Linguini's toque was actually a rat hair!

Anyone Can Cook!

With the Health Inspector sniffing around the kitchen, a famous critic in the restaurant, and a Head Chef determined to ruin them, it's make-or-break time for Remy and Linguini. When Remy is caught by the Health Inspector and Skinner, Linguini looks doomed. But Emile and the rest of the rats have other ideas...

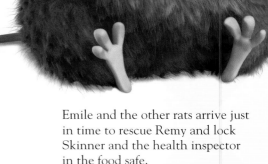

Emile and the other rats arrive just in time to rescue Remy and lock Skinner and the health inspector in the food safe.

The Truth

With no time to spare, Remy must get to the kitchen and help Linguini prepare an extra-special meal for Ego. *Gusteau's* kitchen falls silent as Remy strolls in. Now that everyone knows who the real culinary genius is, will it make a difference?

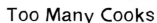

Too Many Cooks

The chefs refuse to accept a rodent as a fellow cook. So, they hand over their toques and aprons and file silently out the back door, leaving *Gusteau's* short-staffed...

Skinner's dream of ruining Linguini collapses like a badly-made soufflé, when Remy and the rats join forces to cook up a happy ending. It's only right that the master chef should eat humble pie and be served his just desserts!

The Boss

As Remy takes charge of the kitchen, Emile and the rats take the place of the kitchen staff. The resulting ratatouille is a triumph and when Ego finds out who's made it, he pronounces him a genius!

"Let's go go go!"

Linguini may finally know that he is Gusteau's son but he is happy not being a chef. He leaves this job to his "little chef".

Call Me Chef

Remy's secret talent proves that Gusteau's famous motto is true—*anyone* can cook. With Ego and Linguini's help, Remy can finally have the future he has always dreamed of.

45

Remy and Linguini's Cooking Tips

"Each flavor is unique!"

Easy Does It

Time to flip it!

That's one perfect pancake!

Tip: *When learning to cook try starting with easy-to-make foods.*

The humble pancake (or crêpe as the French call it) is one of Linguini's favorite recipes. Pancakes are so quick and easy to make that even Linguini can do it, with a little help from Remy, of course. Flipping pancakes is fun, too, although it's easier to do it with big human hands than little rat paws.

Presentation

Tip: Look is as important as taste.

Every top chef knows that how a dish looks is almost as important as how it tastes. A stylish drizzle of dressing and a dollop of caviar give this dish the perfect finishing touch. Delicieux!

To create a stylish drizzle, chefs need a steady hand!

Always have a spoon ready for a taste check.

Remy's nose can always sniff out the best ingredients.

Ingredients

Tip: Always use the freshest herbs and spices you can find.

Top chefs expect the best. Remy is a natural forager, so his talents for sourcing out ingredients help to make all of his dishes a hit.

Eat Good Food

Tip: You are what you eat.

Most rats are like Emile. He doesn't know the meaning of the phrase "healthy eating" and is quite happy to eat unidentifiable garbage. That's why Remy goes out of his way to get his paws on fresh, wholesome ingredients. Whether you're rodent or human his message is the same—don't eat garbage!

Senior Editor Catherine Saunders
Designers Lynne Moulding and Dan Bunyan
Brand Manager Lisa Lanzarini
Publishing Manager Simon Beecroft
Category Publisher Siobhan Williamson
Production Amy Bennett

First published in the United States in 2007 by
DK Publishing
375 Hudson Street
New York, New York 10014

07 08 09 10 11 10 9 8 7 6 5 4 3 2 1
RD140 – 04/07

DK Books are available at special discounts when purchased in
bulk for sales promotions, premiums, fund-raising, or educational use.
For details, contact:DK Publishing Special Markets,
375 Hudson Street, New York, New York 10014
SpecialSales@dk.com

A catalog record for this book is available
from the Library of Congress.

ISBN: 978-0-7566-2991-5

Reproduced by Media Development and Printing Ltd., UK
Printed and bound by Lake Book Manufacturing, Inc. , USA

Acknowledgments:
The publisher would like to thank Leeann Alameda, Mark Andrews, Graham Barnard,
Mary Beech, Kelly Bonbright, Kathleen Chanover, Ed Chen, David Eisenmann, Tony
Fejeran, Cherie Hammond, Laura Hitchcock, Desiree Mourad, Jeff Raymond, Burt
Peng, Victoria Saxon, Krista Sheffler, Muriel Tebid, Clay Welch, and Timothy Zohr.
A special thank you to Lisa Stock for help with proofreading.

Discover more at
www.dk.com